Terrific TRAINS

For Mandy, John, Chloe, and Charlie—T.M.
For Gorran—A.P.

ISBN 0-439-25420-5

Text copyright © 1998 by Tony Mitton.
Illustrations copyright © 1998 by Ant Parker.
All rights reserved.
Published by Scholastic Inc., 555 Broadway, New York, NY 10012,
by arrangement with Larousse Kingfisher Chambers Inc.
SCHOLASTIC and associated logos are trademarks and/or registered
trademarks of Scholastic Inc.

12 11 10 9 8 7 6 5 4 3 2 1   0 1 2 3 4 5/0

Printed in the U.S.A.   23

First Scholastic printing, November 2000

Terrific
TRAINS

Tony Mitton
and
Ant Parker

SCHOLASTIC INC.
New York Toronto London Auckland Sydney
Mexico City New Delhi Hong Kong

Big trains, small trains, old trains and new,

rattling and whistling—Choo, Choo, Choo!

Starting from the station with a whistle and a hiss,

steam trains huffing and puffing like this.

Diesel trains rushing as they rattle down the line,

warning us they're coming with a long, low whine.

Metal wheels whirl as they whizz along the track.
They shimmer and they swish
with a slick click-clack.

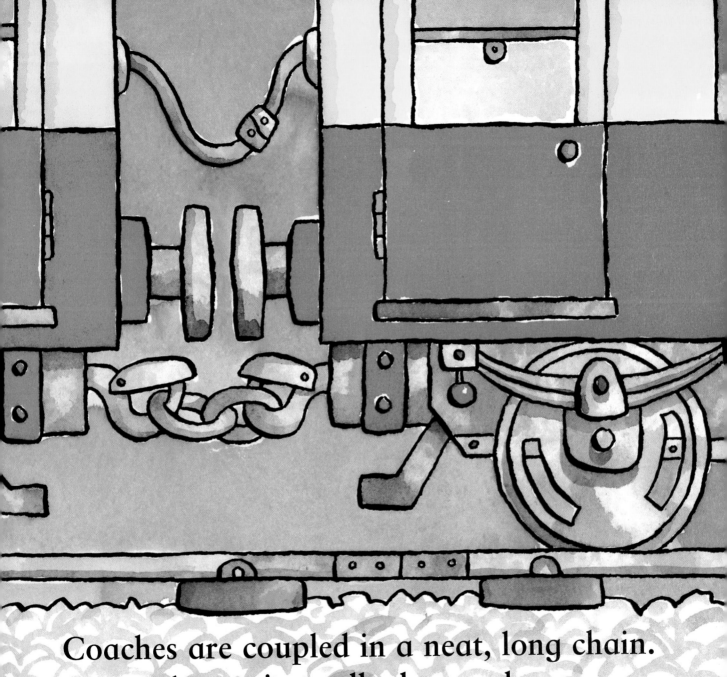

Coaches are coupled in a neat, long chain.
An engine pulls the coaches,
and that makes a train.

If a train meets a river or a valley or a ridge,

the coaches rumble over on a big, strong bridge.

If a train meets a mountain it doesn't have to stop.

It travels through a tunnel and your ears go pop!

When too many trains try to share the same track,

the signals and the switches have to hold some back.

When the rail meets a road,
there's a crossing with a gate.

The train rushes through
while the traffic has to wait.

Trains travel anytime, even very late.

This train's delivering a big load of freight.

This train's for passengers,
it's ready at the station.

All aboard and wave goodbye—
we're going on vacation!

Train parts

rails

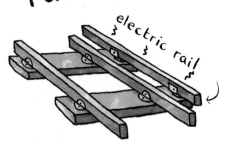

electric rail

these are metal strips that form a pathway called a **track** or **railroad line**. Some trains get their power from an electric rail

whistle

this makes a noise to warn everyone that the train is coming

freight car

this is for carrying goods, called **freight**

signal

this tells engineers when to stop and go

coach

this is for carrying people, called **passengers**

switches

these are the short rails that move to let a train switch from one track to another